KEEPSAKE CRAFTS

WREATHS

WREATHS

KEEPSAKE CRAFTS

GLORIA NICOL

SUNSET PUBLISHING CORPORATION

MENLO PARK, CALIFORNIA

CONTENTS

A QUARTO BOOK

First Printing June 1995

ISBN 0-376-04261-3

Library of Congress Catalog Card Number:
94-068455

For more information on Keepsake Crafts
Wreaths or any other Sunset Book, call
1-800-634-3095.

This book was designed and produced by
Quarto Inc.
The Old Brewery
6 Blundell Street
London N7 9BH

Editor Joanne Jessop
Managing editor Anna Clarkson
Designers Peter Bridgewater /
Ron Bryant-Funnell
Photographer Heini Schneebeli
Illustrator Tony Masero
Art director Moira Clinch
Editorial director Sophie Collins

Manufactured in Hong Kong by
Regent Publishing Services Ltd
Printed in China by
Leefung-Asco Printers Ltd

INTRODUCTION

The craft of wreath-making is steeped in meaning and symbolism. Almost every ancient culture worshiped trees as symbols of divine energy. Evergreens, because they kept their leaves even through the dead of winter, were thought to possess special powers of eternal life. Branches of evergreens were exchanged as symbolic gifts conferring good health, and, to make the branches more decorative, they were bent around to form a wreath.

The wreath was also a form of head-dress. In fact, the word "crown" derives from the Latin word corona, meaning garland or wreath. The ancient Greeks crowned their champion athletes with wreaths of olive, laurel, and myrtle branches, which became symbols of triumph and excellence. During the Olympic games, the host city would

religious holidays and to commemorate special events. For example, when a woman accepted the advances of a lover, she gave him a crown of birch; but if she rejected him, she gave him a crown of

award wreaths made from local trees. The Romans, following in the Greek tradition, crowned their military and athletic heroes with garlands of oak and laurel leaves.

By the sixteenth century, Europeans had adopted the tradition of wearing wreaths in honor of

hazel. Wreaths, whose circular shapes symbolize eternity, were considered fitting adornments at funerals.

Today, hanging a Christmas wreath on the front door is a well-established custom, but using wreaths to decorate our homes is a fairly recent innovation.

of the wreath does not have to conform to tradition; it can be square, oval or heart-shaped. Wreaths can also be used in innovative ways – to decorate the crown of a straw hat, as part of a bridesmaid's headdress, or as a table centerpiece. The options are limitless.

INTRODUCTION

Decorative wreaths can be made with a wide variety of fresh flowers and foliage, or for long-lasting displays, from dried materials. Wreaths that incorporate useful items such as herbs and spices or gardening paraphernalia make practical as well as attractive gifts. The actual shape

In this book you will find many inspiring ideas for creating your own wreaths. There are wreaths that celebrate **the** changing seasons; elegant formal wreaths; whimsical wreaths to delight young children; festive wreaths; functional wreaths that feature practical items; and, of course, wreaths that are purely decorative.

MATERIALS

WREATH BASES

The starting point for any wreath is the base, or frame. The type of base to use depends on whether the wreath materials are fresh or dry and on the size and weight of the finished wreath.

will show through and become part of the overall design.

2 Bases of florist's foam can be used with fresh or dried materials. They are easy to use; just push the plant stems into the foam until the base is completely covered.

3 Swag cage frames filled with blocks of florist's foam can be joined together into longer lengths for garlands and swags or made into circles for wreaths. Use these frames in the same way as foam bases.

4 Wire wreath frames are available in many sizes and when bound with damp sphagnum moss make a

substantial base for any fresh materials. The moss-clad frame can also be left to dry out to use with dried flowers.

5 Single wire rings make a good base for delicately shaped wreaths. They can be lightly padded with moss or simply bound with ribbon to complement the colors of the wreath decor. You can make your own wire rings or buy wire rings used for making lampshades.

1 Circles of twigs or vine, which can be bought or made from scratch, make useful bases for dried materials. If the base is not to be completely covered with material, it

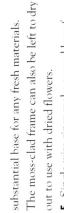

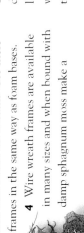

MOSS

Sphagnum moss is used to cover wire bases when making wreaths with fresh plant materials.

Soaking the moss in water for a few hours beforehand provides a damp base for insertion of the stems and helps to keep the finished wreath looking fresh.

Carpet or bun moss is much denser and greener than sphagnum moss and comes in flat pieces. Its rich velvety texture gives it a more decorative quality.

WIRES, TWINES & TAPES

There are many gauges of wire available for floral work, so you can match the thickness of wire to the materials you will be using.

Stub wires come in various lengths and are used for attaching fruits, cones and flowers to the wreath.

Reel wire comes on a continuous spool and is used for binding moss to a frame and other general uses. The finest reel wires can be used to bind together delicate materials such as brittle dried flowers or fine fresh flowers such as lilies-of-the-valley and grape hyacinths.

Garden twine is available in reels and balls and comes in green or brown. It is useful for binding the moss to a wreath frame and can also be used decoratively to tie materials together in small bundles.

Florist's tape is a rubber-coated tape used to cover the wires in the false stems of dried and fresh flowers.

GENERAL TOOLS

Florist's scissors are essential for cutting stems and can also be used to cut wires. Pruning shears are needed to cut the woody stems on foliage.

An electric glue gun is a worthwhile, though not essential, investment. Heavy items such as nuts and pine cones can be fastened securely in place with hot glue, which sets in a matter of seconds. Choose general purpose glue sticks for wreath making.

A plant sprayer is useful for refreshing fresh flowers and foliage.

9

BASIC TECHNIQUES

MOSS BASES

Damp moss covering a wire frame is ideal for a wreath made with fresh plants. Wire frames can be bought from florists and nurseries and come in a variety of sizes, with either flat or angled sides. Remember that the finished wreath will be much fuller than the original ring when all the moss, foliage and decorative material has been added.

To make the moss base, soak sphagnum moss in water for several hours, then gently squeeze out the excess water. Open out the moss, place a handful on the top side of the wire frame and bind it on with reel wire or garden twine that has been twisted or tied around the frame to secure it. Continue adding moss and binding it in place until the frame is completely covered. Then secure the end of the wire or twine firmly to the frame.

For a more delicate frame, bend a wire coat hanger into a circle and pad it lightly with moss in the same way.

To retain their freshness as long as possible, keep the wreaths cool and spray with water every day.

VINE BASES

Vine or twig bases can be bought ready-made and are reasonably inexpensive. You can make your own using virtually any type of pliable twigs or vines, although wisteria, honeysuckle and grape are most commonly used.

If the vines are dry, soak them in water until they are flexible and easy to work with. Pick out a few stems and, holding them together, bend them around to form a ring of the required size. If the vines are too short, just add in other stems, staggering, twisting and overlapping the ends until they all hold together when bent into a ring.

Holding the vine circle in one hand, begin to wrap a long piece of vine around the ring, capturing shorter pieces as you go. For a vine base with more volume, add additional vines and wrap them in the same direction.

WIRING THE MATERIALS

Bunches of foliage, fruits and flowers need to be wired with stub wires before attaching them to wreath bases.

1 To attach soft fruits such as apples, limes and pomegranates to a wreath, push a stub wire through the fruit a quarter of the way up from its base, then twist the wire together, leaving one long end. Push another wire through the fruit at right angles to the first, twisting them together in the same way. Finally, twist the two long ends together.

2 To wire a pine cone, wrap a piece of stub wire around the base as close to the bottom and as far inside the cone as possible, leaving a long end sticking out.

3 To prepare nuts such as walnuts and brazil nuts, push a piece of stub wire into the eye of each nut and dot with glue to secure. For other types of nuts, wind the end of a stub wire to make a tiny flat loop, then glue it to the nut.

4 For a seed head with a stem, wrap the end of a piece of stub wire around the stem several times and leave a long end. For a seed head without a stem, glue a wire loop to the head.

5 Wiring flowers and leaves is necessary when the stems are delicate or if the flower heads are to be contoured or angled into a precise position. Wiring can strengthen the materials and make them much more pliable.

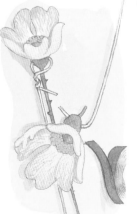

6 To wire a flower head, cut the stem to just a few inches long and push a stub wire horizontally through the base of the flower. Bend the pieces of wire down and twist them around the stem several times. Cut off one end, to leave a single wire stem, and cover the wire with florist's tape.

To wire a bow, tie it and push a stub wire through the back, twist the ends together and trim off any excess, leaving a long end to attach the bow to the wreath.

SPRING

This is the season of rejuvenation and new
beginnings. As spring gets underway and the
days become warmer, there is a feeling of optimism
and excitement and the garden comes alive. Spring
flowers such as delicate snowdrops, narcissus and
hyacinths provide a rich array of colors that can be
combined to make beautiful floral wreaths. If fresh
materials are not plentiful, try using interesting
alternatives such as foil-wrapped candies or corrugated
cardboard to make unusual wreaths that reflect the
exuberance of the spring season.

GARDENING WREATH

Wreaths can be useful as well as

purely decorative. A wreath with a

gardening theme makes an ideal gift

for somebody with a green thumb

because most of the materials used

to decorate the wreath can

also be put to good use

in the garden.

Colorful packages of plant seeds, garden twine, plant labels and tiny terra-cotta flower pots are easy to find at hardware stores and nurseries. A small trowel or gardening gloves could also be included in your gardening wreath. When you have selected your wreath decorations, attach stub wire to them.

Terra-cotta pots with holes in the bottom are easy to attach with wire threaded through the holes.

14

Bind the seed packages with natural raffia and then twist a piece of stub wire around the raffia at the back of each package, leaving a long end of wire to attach to the wreath base.

Make small bundles of twine, tied in the middle to stop them from unraveling. Thread stub wire through the back of each bundle.

Arrange the decorations on the base before attaching them firmly in place by pushing and twisting all the stub wire ends through to the back of the base and threading them in and out of the twigs a few times. Small decorative metal watering cans and terra-cotta plant pots filled with moss add a colorful touch to this gardening wreath.

This gardening wreath has a rustic twig base and all the materials are attached with wire.

NARCISSUS & IVY WREATH

Paper white narcissus, one of the first flowers of spring, appears in even the most inclement weather to herald the beginning of the gardening season.

A simple wreath made from bunches of these delicate white flowers looks particularly fresh when offset by contrasting dark green ivy leaves.

Prepare the base for this wreath by placing handfuls of damp sphagnum moss, which have been soaked in water for a few hours beforehand, around a small wire frame. Use garden twine to hold the moss in place (see Basic Techniques). Cut the ends of the narcissus stems diagonally.

Working in one direction, place the ivy leaves and narcissi on the frame so that they overlap and their stems push lightly into the damp moss. Bend small pieces of stub wire into U shapes and push them over the stems through the moss to the back of the wreath to hold everything firmly in place.

An ivy wreath

sprinkled with

delicate white

flowers brings

a touch of spring

into the house.

HYACINTH WREATH

Blue and white is a fresh and vibrant color combination
for a spring flower wreath of hyacinths.

This wreath calls for the same type of moss-covered wire frame as the one used for the narcissus and ivy wreath. Push short sprigs of laurustinus into the moss, working around the circle in the same direction to cover the base and provide a lush background for the flowers. Bend short pieces of stub wire into U shapes and push them over the stems to hold the laurustinus in place.

Before adding the flowers, cut the stems diagonally. Arrange the blue hyacinths around the wreath among the laurustinus. Push the stems into the moss and hold them in place with wire. Follow the same procedure for the white hyacinths, dotting them around the circle among the foliage and blue hyacinths.

To keep your fresh flower wreaths looking good for as long as possible, spray the flowers, foliage and moss base regularly with water.

The exquisite-

looking wreath

shown here has an

added bonus – the

sweet scent of

hyacinths.

WOODLAND EGG WREATH

Deep green carpet moss makes a sumptuous base for a woodland wreath that incorporates catkins and pretty speckled quail eggs.

This woodland egg wreath is decorated with small speckled quail eggs. Make sure that the eggs have been kept at room temperature for several hours beforehand. Pierce both ends of the egg with a sharp needle, then push the needle carefully through the hole to break up the egg inside. Holding the egg over a dish, gently blow out the yolk and white. Wash out each blown egg with a disinfectant, rinse it well and let dry. Make platforms for the eggs to sit on by bending the ends of stub wires into small flat loops. Glue the quail eggs securely onto the wire platforms.

To make the wreath, bind a wire frame with damp sphagnum moss in the usual way (see Basic Techniques). Cover the top side of the base with large pieces of carpet moss and hold them in place with short U-shaped pieces of wire pushed down into the moss around the edges. Arrange small bunches of forget-me-nots around the

circle; push the stems into the moss and pin them in position with wires. Add some catkins, pushing the stems into the moss. Finally, add dried mushrooms and quail eggs and wire them in place. Yellow and white checked bows complete this delightful woodland design.

18

FOIL-WRAPPED CANDY WREATH

Stunning wreaths can be made from everyday materials.

Colorful foil-wrapped candies combined with tiny fluted baking cups make an interesting decorative wreath that resembles Mexican folk art.

The base for this wreath is a standard wire frame that has been pressed and flattened slightly to reduce the angle of the sides. The frame is then covered with metallic cardboard. In order to shape the cardboard to fit the frame, roll the frame slowly over the cardboard and mark the inside and outside edges with a pencil as you go. This makes it easier to fit the cardboard onto the frame. Tie it onto the frame with ribbon slotted through slits cut along the inner and outer edges of the cardboard.

Arrange oval and round fluted baking cups around the circle and fasten them in place with a glue gun. Glue a candy inside each baking cup. Glue longer, thin-shaped candies to fill the gaps between the baking cups. Tie short pieces of cord around the long thin candies and thread the cord through holes made with an awl in the cardboard. Tie the cord into knots and trim the ends.

CARDBOARD WREATH

Wreaths made from the simplest materials can give surprisingly stylish results.

This oval wreath is decorated with scrolls made from smooth cardboard and acanthus leaves made from chunky corrugated cardboard. The colors have been kept simple – a combination of white and natural – and the different textures have been deliberately placed side by side. The wreath is so elegant it could double as a frame for a picture or mirror. It would also look good sprayed gold, enhancing the classical style of the design.

To make the oval wreath base, first draw a pattern on paper. For an even shape, start by drawing a quarter of the oval onto a piece of paper folded into quarters, then transpose this quarter onto the other three parts. Copy the oval pattern on

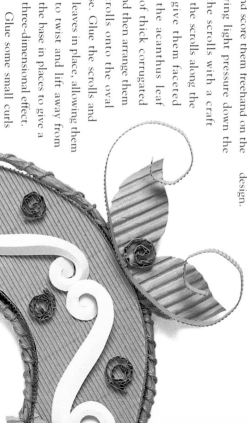

a piece of fine corrugated cardboard, then cut it out. Cut thin strips of cardboard and stick them in place around the inner and outer edges of the oval to give it depth.

Cut the scrolls out of smooth white cardboard and score them freehand on the front, applying light pressure down the middle of the scrolls with a craft knife. Bend the scrolls along the scoring to give them faceted sides. Cut the acanthus leaf shapes out of thick corrugated cardboard and then arrange them with the scrolls onto the oval base. Glue the scrolls and leaves in place, allowing them to twist and lift away from the base in places to give a three-dimensional effect.

Glue some small curls of rolled-up corrugated

cardboard into the spaces between the shapes. Finish the inner and outer side edges by gluing on rolled-up cardboard or paper raffia bound with string. Place an acanthus leaf with curled bands and a small curl made from corrugated cardboard at the top of the wreath to complete the design.

A spicy wreath makes a pleasant and practical decoration for your kitchen. The choice of decorative spices is a matter of personal taste.

CHILE & PEPPERCORN WREATH

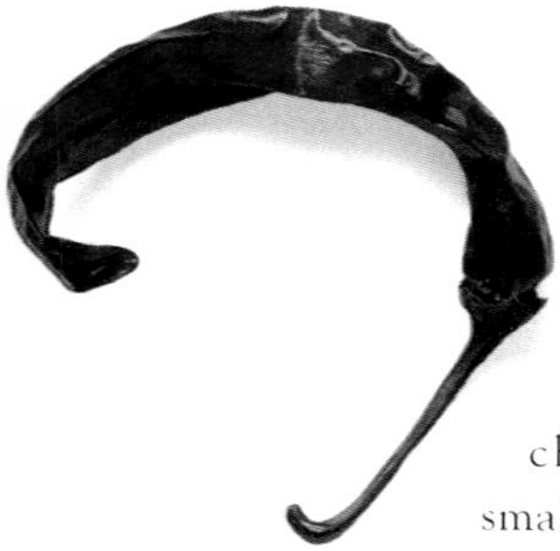

A ring of dried chile peppers and small bunches of pink peppercorns provide interesting shapes and colors for this hot spicy wreath, which would look good in any country kitchen. Try adding more spices to make practical and aromatic variations;

whole garlic heads, and small cheesecloth bags of cloves, coriander seeds and cardamom pods are ideal.

The wreath shown here uses a ready-made natural-colored wreath base with overlapping corn husks. It is very simple but provides plenty of interest and texture for this spicy display.

A corn-husk wreath

base provides a

rustic look.

Position the dried chile peppers around the base, pointing in the same direction around the circle. Be sure to leave gaps for the peppercorns between the chiles and at the top for the bow.

Pink peppercorns are very fragile and require gentle handling. Make small bunches of peppercorns by twisting very fine stub wire around their brittle stems. Incorporate a thicker stub wire among the stems to give each bunch a strong pointed end to push in between the corn husks and to hold the peppercorn bunches onto the wreath. Push each bunch into position, then glue the chiles in place using a glue gun. Make a bow from wire-edged ribbon and attach it to the wreath.

SUMMER

During the long days of summer, the garden is permeated with the fragrances and glorious colors of flowers. At the height of the growing season there is a lush variety of plant life available for fresh wreaths. Or you can dry the summer blooms for wreath-making later in the year. Summer is also the season for vacations at the beach, beachcombing and lazing in the sun. Mementoes of the sun and the ocean can be incorporated into a special wreath that will keep pleasant vacation memories alive all through the year.

A wreath frame made of pale twigs gives a natural windswept and sun-bleached look to this shell wreath. Wind several long strands of raffia around the base. Start by tying the raffia around one strand of wood on the back of the twig base and finish by securing the ends and trimming away any excess, but without making it too neat.

Shells, with their

intricate shapes

and patterns make

a lovely display.

Dried seaweed, and

bits of driftwood

complete the

maritime

theme.

SHELL WREATH

A wreath made of seashells and other bits and pieces

that have washed ashore helps to keep alive

those pleasant memories of trips to the

beach on warm summer days.

Arrange shells, dried seaweed, starfish and small pieces of driftwood around the wreath base in groups, with spaces between for the base to show through. Glue them in place using a glue gun. A piece of driftwood, bound and tied with strands of raffia, is wired at the top of the wreath. The ends of the raffia are allowed to curl and dangle down naturally into the center of the ring.

The padded animal shapes can be permanently stitched to the base or fastened on with Velcro so they can be removed and played with as toys.

Use a narrow twig base and wrap it with a bias-cut strip of ticking fabric 1½ inches wide. Make the strip by stitching together shorter pieces of fabric. When the base is covered, stitch the strip in place at the back of the base.

Make paper patterns of simple animal shapes – a puppy, a rabbit, an elephant, and a teddy bear – with a small seam allowance around each one. Using these patterns, cut the animal shapes out of scraps of brightly colored checkered fabrics; allow two pieces for each animal. With right sides of the fabric together, stitch each pair of shapes around the edges, leaving a hole for the padding. Cut the seam allowances along the curves before turning right side out. Stuff the animals lightly with a washable polyester padding, which helps to soften the shapes. When padded, sew up the hole. Stitch a tiny bow to the neck of each animal.

Place the animals around the wreath and fasten them in place with small pieces of Velcro® stitched to the backs of each of them and in corresponding positions on the wreath. Alternatively, stitch the animals directly onto the base.

28

CHILD'S FOLK ART WREATH

For a child's wreath with folk art charm, simply use up scraps of homespun checkered fabrics and striped ticking fabric. This makes an ideal decoration for a child's bedroom.

This rich green wreath can be made with your favorite herbs from the garden.

KITCHEN HERB WREATH

Cover a wire frame with damp moss and bind in place with twine (see Basic Techniques). Trim herbs with woody stems into 4 inch pieces, cutting the stems diagonally so that the ends are pointed. Gather the softer stemmed varieties, such as sage and thyme, into small bunches, using florist's wire with an end left pointing out for attaching to the wreath.

Arrange the herbs around the moss base so that they face in one direction all the way around. Push the pointed stems directly into the moss, and push the wires on the bunches through to the back of the frame and wind around to secure. Wire a bow to the wreath to finish.

The ingredients for a kitchen wreath can be removed when needed and new herbs and spices added to fill in the bare spots. Use a combination of herbs, choosing a good mix of colors and textures; the wreath shown here uses bay leaves, rosemary, thyme and purple sage.

A wreath made from fresh herbs and hung near the stove makes a useful, aromatic decoration for the kitchen. It will continue to look good as it dries out naturally.

COTTAGE GARDEN WREATH

Cottage garden flowers perfectly capture the spirit of midsummer, and many of these blooms can easily be dried for displaying when the season is over.

Always pick the flowers on a clear sunny morning, after the dew has evaporated, choosing well-shaped and blemish-free heads that are not too open. Find a warm place with good ventilation for drying. Hang the flowers upside-down to dry in small bunches; keeping them away from bright light helps to retain their rich colors. This summer wreath is made from a sumptuous mixture of pink and blue flowers – lavender, peonies, love-lies-bleeding, rose-buds, globe thistle, lark-

spur, and love-in-a-mist – with eucalyptus and sage leaves for foliage.

A circle of dry florist's foam makes an ideal firm base for a dry flower wreath. Cut the eucalyptus into short pieces and push them into the foam, working in one direction around the wreath and allowing some of the leaves to break out naturally around the edges of the frame. Carefully wire the sage and lavender into small bunches with fine florist's wire. Push the bundles in between the eucalyptus stems.

Next, push the large peony heads and the remaining blooms into position, placing them at random to fill in all the gaps for a dense effect. Wire a bow to the top of the wreath to finish.

VEGETABLE
WREATH

A crop of miniature vegetables, freshly picked from the kitchen garden, can be turned into a delightful wreath.

These everyday foods take on an ornamental quality when arranged to emphasize their subtle coloring and markings. Baby artichokes, eggplants, and asparagus can also be included in this vegetable wreath, as well as pink turnips, tiny ears of corn, and even a small cabbage or cauliflower.

All the vegetables must be wired for attaching to the wreath (see Basic Techniques). Push pieces of stub wire through the vegetables, then twist together leaving a long end. Gather smaller items such as radishes and Brussels sprouts into bunches and asparagus spears into bundles with a few twists of fine wire.

Cover the wire with twine or raffia and tie the ends in a knot. Wrap a wire frame with some damp sphagnum moss and bind it with twine (see Basic Techniques). Cover the frame with a foliage background of laurustinus interspersed with sprigs of rosemary. Push the stems into the moss, working in one direction around the ring.

Arrange the vegetables in groups among the foliage, pushing the wires through the moss to the back and twisting the ends a couple of times around the frame. A bow provides a finishing detail.

Vegetables in

various shapes,

sizes, and colors

have been

arranged in

groups.

Cabbage leaves add

beautifully subtle

textures to a

wreath.

ROSE WREATH

A continuous ring of fresh roses interspersed with bits of foliage celebrates summer at its best.

For this wreath, old-fashioned garden roses or long-stemmed roses give a softer, more natural look than the hybrid tea roses or floribunda types.

Rosebuds worked onto a single wire frame and allowed to dry and fade naturally result in a long-lasting circlet that has its own special beauty. Alternatively, full-blown roses will give a spectacular but fleeting effect since they are likely to drop their petals as they dry.

Wire each rose by cutting the stem to about one and a half inches and pushing a piece of stub wire horizontally through the base of the flower head. Bend and wind the wire down over the

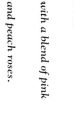

natural stem, to create a false stem. Cover this new flexible stem with florist's tape. Buds and spray roses need to be wired into small bunches.

After wiring all the roses, wind them onto a single-wire base, working in one direction around it and interspersing the flower heads with foliage.

This lovely summer

wreath was made

with a blend of pink

and peach roses.

33

SACHET WREATH

Lavender sachets that bring their sweet fragrance to the linen closet can also

be used to decorate wreaths that perfume the rest of your home.

The sachets on this wreath were made with small pieces of checkered Madras cotton fabric, which comes in wonderfully mellow color combinations.

Use a plain wooden vine base to give a rustic feel to this sachet wreath. Wind strings of metal leaves (with wire stems and a bright verdigris finish) around the base, then twist and arrange the leaves at different angles around the circle. Other leafy coverings, such as dried stems

of long-leaved eucalyptus, can be used instead, but the overall look should be kept sparse and simple.

For each lavender sachet, cut out a fabric rectangle measuring 6 inches by 5 inches; this includes a half-inch seam allowance. Fold the rectangle in half lengthwise, with the right sides of the fabric facing together, and stitch the open side and bottom edges. Trim the seam allowance and turn the fabric right side out

to make a small bag. Turn the open unfinished edge at the top of the bag to the inside and iron the folded edge flat, making a sachet that is approximately 4 inches deep.

Fill each bag two-thirds full with dried lavender flowers and tie a ribbon around to close up the top. Push a piece of stub wire through the fabric on the back of each sachet; twist the wire around itself to leave a long end. Push the wire through the wreath base to the back and carefully wrap it around one thickness of vine.

A string of metal

leaves provides

an added touch.

Little sachets of lavender in checkered

Madras fabric give this simple summer

wreath an unmistakable feel of the country.

Choose colors that blend with your

furnishings.

FALL

The fall, with its subtle shades of gold, brown, russet and bronze and its rich harvest of berries and fruits, provides plenty of inspiration for wreath making. Fall wreaths that feature dried flowers, seed heads, fruits, and berries set against burnished foliage or honey-colored wheat capture the essence of this mellow season of harvest and will lend a touch of warmth during the cold months ahead.

HARVEST SQUARE WREATH

A wreath of golden wheat and other fruits of the field

celebrates the rich bounty of harvest time.

The fall harvest wreath follows the British tradition of the corn dolly, which is a small figure made from dried wheat. Farmers used to make corn dollies to keep the spirit of the harvested field safe throughout the long winter, ready to be released again in the spring.

The square frame is an unusual alternative and could be used to frame a mirror or sit on a shelf. To make the frame, arrange a square of four woody sticks with their ends crossed, then bind the corners with some garden twine. Cover the sticks with some sphagnum moss

and bind it on with twine (see Basic Techniques). Allow the moss to dry out thoroughly before decorating.

Wire dried golden wheat into small bundles, leaving a long end of wire. Trim the bundles neatly, then cover the wires with garden twine and tie it into a knot. Arrange the bundles of wheat around the frame, leaving a space at the top, and fasten them to the frame by wrapping the stub wires around the sticks. Wire together a few dried sunflower heads and attach them to the wreath at the top. Create a focal point with a flourish of ribbon in seasonal tones.

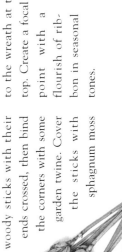

Dried wheat

and sunflowers

capture the essence

of fall.

DRIED FLOWER WREATH

Dried fall fruits and flowers were mixed together to produce this mellow color combination.

Dried flowers,

pods, and seed

heads are featured

in this fall wreath.

Make a foundation for this dried flower wreath by bending supple tree branches (we've used twisted hazel) together into a ring. Extra branches can be added when necessary, but allow the wispy ends to curl outward around the sides of the wreath base.

To dry the hydrangeas, hang them upside-down in a warm place. Covering the flower heads with a paper bag helps to retain their color. Alternatively, leave the hydrangeas in a jug of water until the water has evaporated. Dry pomegranates by storing them in a warm place until they dry out.

Group dried pomegranates, dried hydrangeas, seed heads, and pods on the base, allowing gaps for the woody base to show through. Push wires through the fruits and flower heads and wind them around the stems. Then fasten the pomegranates and hydrangeas onto the frame. Glue the seed heads and pods in place, using a glue gun. Finally, tie a taffeta ribbon bow and wire it to the bottom of the wreath.

A circle of autumn leaves adorned with larch cones creates

a wreath with a classical feel.

OAK LEAF WREATH

Working with dry, brittle leaves can be extremely tricky and calls for a light and delicate touch.

Prewire each oak leaf by gluing a short piece of fine reel wire to the back of each leaf. Carefully twist one end of the wire a few times around the stem. Then arrange the oak leaves around a wire ring frame, leaving spaces between them. Secure the leaves by winding the other end of each wire around the wreath frame to

hold the leaf in position. Cut off any excess wire.

When you have completed the circle of leaves, glue a short piece of fine reel wire near the base of each larch cone and attach to the wreath. Secure everything in place with small blobs of glue over the wires on the underside of the frame.

41

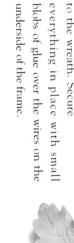

BERRY WREATH

Fall brings with it an abundance of richly colored foliage and branches heavy with fruits and berries.

Decorate a wreath with a fall bouquet of rosehips, brambles, and viburnum gathered from the forests and countryside. Berries and foliage, especially those varieties with leathery leaves, will hold up well in cool conditions for about three weeks. Both berries and leaves will shrink slightly as they dry out, but they should still hold their color. Spraying with water each day will help the wreath to last longer.

To make a berry wreath, bend branches of pyracantha around a vine base, with the leaves and bunches of berries facing the front. Secure the branches with garden raffia. Add other foliage with berries to fill out the wreath and add color and texture. Cut stems of eucalyptus with frothy pinkish fruits into short sprays, push them in among the pyracantha, and fasten in place with wires twisted around the base. Add bunches of spindle berries and spiky stems of myrtle.

Another method of making a berry wreath is to cut a wreath out of thin plywood. Layer branches of foliage and berries around the base so they all face in one direction with the leaves of each branch covering the stems of the branch next to it. Staple the branches to the base with a staple gun. Attach a picture hook on the back of the frame to hang the wreath.

Rosy red berries set against a glossy green background give a feeling of warmth and cheer to this garland of leathery leaves.

A pretty lavender wreath draped casually over a lampshade is a lovely sight and an unusual way to display a flower arrangement.

LAVENDER LAMPSHADE WREATH

The color and sweet fragrance of lavender has a timeless appeal.

A profusion of a

single type of

flower, such as

lavender, makes

a beautifully

simple wreath.

A simple wreath made from aromatic lavender flowers is an elegant way to decorate a lampshade. A single wire ring used for making lampshades is ideal for the wreath frame. Choose a size that will sit comfortably one half to one third of the way down your lampshade. Please remember that dried material is flammable so the wreath should not be left for long periods when the lamp is switched on.

Gather together small bunches of dried lavender on long stems; twist fine reel wire a few times around the stems just below the flower heads, leaving a long end of wire. Trim all the stems to make bunches that are approximately 4 inches in length. Working around the outer edge of the ring frame, bind the lavender bunches onto the frame one by one with each bunch facing the same direction and the flowers overlapping the stems of the bunch next to it. When the wreath is completely covered, tie a piece of ribbon around it, making a bow that has long trailing ends.

Citrus fruits add their bright colorings and distinctive scent

to a simple wreath of glossy green bay leaves.

DRIED CITRUS WREATH

Gather fresh bay leaves into bunches and wire the stems together with fine reel wire. Bind the bunches onto a twig base by wrapping natural raffia over the stems. Point all the bay leaf bunches the same direction and place each bunch with the leaves over-

lapping the stems of the previous bunch. When the wreath is completely clad with bay leaves, thread dried orange slices into groups of five or six on pieces of raffia with the ends brought together and tied into bows. Fasten these circles onto the wreath with wire. Wire each lime with two stub wires on each fruit (see Basic Techniques) and fasten in place by twisting the wires around the back of the twig base. Finish off the wreath with a bow made from several strands of raffia.

Dried orange slices can be bought from specialist suppliers, or you can dry them yourself by baking them slowly in the oven at a low temperature until they are hard. Small lemons and kumquats wired into bunches would make attractive and colorful additions.

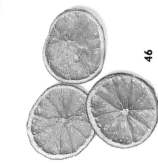

Bay leaves make
a lush base for
orange slices and
small limes.

WINTER

As the cold, stark months of winter settle in, there are the festivities of Christmas and the New Year to look forward to. Festive wreaths help to lift the spirits and add a personal touch to your decorations. The garden may be dormant but there are plenty of evergreens that can be put to good use. Boughs of ivy, holly, and mistletoe make long-lasting wreath bases and are an ideal backdrop for an arrangement of nuts, fir cones, or your favorite Christmas decorations.

STAR WREATH

Decorating the door with a Christmas wreath follows in a tradition that began with the ancient Romans, who exchanged evergreen branches bent into rings to symbolize good health.

This festive green and white star-shaped wreath of eucalyptus, broom, and larch is a modern variation on the traditional ring of evergreen branches.

Make the five-pointed star frame from three wire coat hangers. Measure down from the point on each side of the hanger and cut to the same length using wire cutters. Arrange these wire points to form the star shape, with the wire ends bent back approximately 1 inch, at an angle, so that each end overlaps the next one, forming the star's inside corners. Glue each overlap and bind with wire to hold it firmly together.

Cover the star frame with sphagnum moss bound on with twine (see Basic Techniques). Remember, when making a single wire frame like this, to keep the weight as light as possible at this stage so that the weight of the finished wreath does not pull the frame out of shape.

The green and

white theme of this

star wreath reflects

the subdued colors

of winter.

Cut fine-leaved eucalyptus into short pieces with pointed ends that are easy to push into the moss frame. Place white broom, with stems cut short, in among the eucalyptus, then secure them in place with small U-shaped pieces of stub wire, twisted together at the back of the frame.

Add short twigs of larch and wire them in place. A green bow, attached with wire, adds a nice finishing touch.

As an alternative, decorate your star wreath with white Christmas roses. Their waxy flowers will stay fresh for quite some time. Clusters of cranberries nestled in among the dark green foliage would provide a cheerful color contrast. The red berries could be highlighted with a red bow.

Spools of thread, needles, pins, a thimble and a small pair

of scissors can be used to decorate a sewing wreath for

someone with a passion for needlework.

SEWING WREATH

A tape measure and the spools of thread are tied onto this sewing wreath with ribbon; a thimble holder, a small package of needles, dressmaker's chalk and a pair of tiny scissors all fit nicely into custom-made felt pockets. To make the wreath, cut a ring to the desired finished wreath size out of stiff cardboard and then transfer the shape onto two pieces of fabric. Add an inch around the outside of the front piece; add about three quarters of an inch around the outside of the back piece. Add a half inch seam allowance on the inside of both rings. Cut out the two fabric rings with pinking shears.

Use felt to make the thimble holder, needle case and the pockets to hold the

various sewing tools. Position them on the front piece of the fabric ring. Sew on the bands of thin ribbon, which will be tied around a tape measure and threaded through the spools.

With the right sides of the fabric rings together, stitch around the inside of the circle, about one-half inch from the edge. Trim the seam and snip along the seam allowance to the stitching line. Turn the fabric ring right side out.

Work gathering stitches around the outside of the front of the ring, about three quarters of an inch in from the edge, then gather to fit the back. Glue a layer of padding to the

cardboard ring and insert it into the fabric wreath. Stitch the front to the back, with the pinked edges outside. Finish with a bow made from a band of colored embroidery threads.

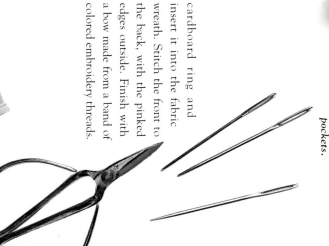

Sewing tools are

attached with

ribbons, felt strips

and custom-made

pockets.

This old-fashioned wreath was first embellished with checkered fabrics and colorful stitching, then decorated with small buttons.

Odd buttons, found in the button box,

can be put to good use to make a

charming fabric wreath with a

homespun feel.

BUTTON WREATH

Simple shapes of checkered fabric are used to appliqué this button wreath.

To make the wreath, first draw a ring onto calico for the front, then draw another ring the same size onto a contrasting fabric for the back. Divide the calico ring into six segments. Cut checkered fabrics to cover three alternate segments and tack them in place. Outline each segment with a band of fabric with the edges turned under. Sew the bands in place with running stitches; use embroidery thread of contrasting colors. Make up patterns for all six segments. Try sewing on squares, hearts, circles and diamond shapes in contrasting fabrics with colorful threads. Cross stitching and feather stitching add to the decorative effect. Sew the buttons on last, in lines along the bands dividing each segment and as focal points on the checkered shapes.

When the decorations are completed, stitch the front and back together around the outer edge, with the right sides of the fabric facing together. Turn the circle to the right side. Fold the raw edges of the

inside circle on both pieces into the wrong side, snipping the curves where necessary. Tack in place, then hand stitch the front and back together, leaving a small opening for the stuffing. Pad the ring lightly with kapok and stitch the hole closed. A bow and hanging loop of grosgrain ribbon completes the wreath.

SILVER PINE CONE WREATH

Shimmering silver pine cones make a spectacular Christmas wreath to decorate

your front door and welcome family and friends during the holiday season.

The wreath shown on the opposite page was made with pine cones that had been sprayed silver and larch branches covered with green lichen. It makes a striking feature in this candlelit corner of the room. The soft pale colors of the larch and lichen are accentuated by the rich reds in the background, while the glow from the candles casts a shimmer over the silvery pine cones.

Prepare a base for this pine cone wreath by binding sphagnum moss onto a wire frame then letting it dry out. Wire each pine cone by wrapping a piece of florist's wire

around the base, as close to the bottom and as far inside the cone as possible, leaving a long end sticking out. Spray all the pine cones with silver paint.

Choose larch twigs clad with green lichen and arrange them around the circular frame, working in the same direction all the way around so the ends jut out naturally around the wreath. Push the twigs into the moss. Where necessary, push small U-shaped pieces of stub wire over the stems

and through the moss to the back of the wreath. Arrange the cones around the wreath. Push the wire ends through to the back, then twist them around the frame to secure the cones.

For a variation, make this wreath with a mixture of different sizes of cones and spray them gold or bronze.

Salt dough is easy

to shape into

cherubs, angels,

and stars for a

long-lasting

decoration.

CHERUB WREATH

In this cherub wreath, golden angels form a celestial circle with a fanfare of trumpets, a cherub's head proudly sits at the top, and stars sprinkle the scene.

The stars and angels that adorn this golden cherub wreath were made out of a malleable dough mixture with a high concentration of salt, which, when baked and painted, lasts almost indefinitely.

To make the salt dough, mix 2 cups of all-purpose flour with 1 cup of salt. Add water gradually to the dry ingredients until the dough is stiff, but not sticky, and knead for ten minutes until it is smooth and manageable. To prevent the salt dough from dry-ing out, keep it tightly wrapped in plastic wrap until ready for

use. Draw outlines for the cherub head, angels and stars on stiff paper or card-board. Using these patterns, cut shapes out of the salt dough. Add pieces of dough to make the wings and angel hair. Use a toothpick to add extra details to the dough figures. Make one large star with a small hole at the top. Bake the dough figures in a slow oven at 200°F for approximately 8 hours, until they are completely dry.

Glue the cherub, angels and stars onto a twig base and spray everything gold. When the paint is dry, thread the large star, also painted gold, with fine cord and attach to the top of the wreath so that it hangs down into the center of the circle.

RIBBON FLOWER WREATH

A wreath of ribbon roses makes a beautiful everlasting decoration with a nostalgic theme. The roses were made with taffeta ribbon in subtle shades of burgundy, red, pink and orange. A long trailing bow in matching ribbon gives this rose wreath an air of opulence and elegance.

Wire-edged taffeta ribbons are ideal for making the flowers because they can be crunched and folded and will hold their shape, but wide grosgrain ribbon or tubes of *doupioni* silk fabric, pressed flat, also work well.

To make the base, wrap moiré ribbon around a small wire wreath frame to cover it completely. Secure the end of the ribbon with a few stitches.

Make a ribbon rose by first cutting a 24-inch length of 1½-inch-wide ribbon. Start the rose by folding one end of the ribbon in half lengthwise, keeping the selvages at the bottom. Turn the ribbon around itself a couple of times to form the

center of the flower. Secure the base with a few stitches. Work along the ribbon, opening it out so that it is no longer folded. Continue pleating, turning and stitching the ribbon at the base as the rose forms. Fold the end of the ribbon to hide it under the base and stitch it in place. Arrange the flowers around the wreath frame and then stitch them in place, finishing off with a long trailing bow.

Try using various color combinations of roses. For a subtle effect, make all the flowers from different shades of one color. Or, for a bold look, make the roses out of two strongly contrasting colors, such as red and white. Varying the rose sizes would also be effective.

This ribbon rose wreath was made with a blend of soft, warm colors.

The darker-colored roses can be complemented by a dark bow.

Hearts are a popular motif in the folk art of

many countries, so a heart-shaped wreath

has universal appeal. Made from seasonal

materials, it can decorate the home at any

time of year, but it is especially appropriate as a Valentine's gift.

HEART-SHAPED WREATH

The base for this heart wreath consists of a shallow heart-shaped cardboard box. The box was filled with green shredded paper to create a background for a cluster of pink rose buds that form another, smaller heart in the center of the larger heart shape. The entire wreath was then framed with a row of copper beech leaves.

To make the box, draw a heart shape onto thick cardboard. Take strips of thinner cardboard and bend them around the heart and glue them in place. Cover the seams and reinforce the base and sides with masking tape. Completely cover the sides with tape and then fold the tape over the

sides and into the box. Spread some glue over the inside of the heart-shaped box. Scrunch up some green shredded paper and push it into the box to provide a soft background for the rose heart.

Group the rose buds on top of the shredded paper so that they form a smaller

heart shape that exactly duplicates the heart shape of the box. Then arrange a border of copper beech leaves around the base of the box and glue them in place. Add a double bow of satin ribbon to the top of the heart.

This box of hearts and roses makes a *perfect Valentine's Day wreath.*

ACKNOWLEDGMENTS

The author would like to thank Emma Hardy for all her help making the wreaths and Caroline Alexander of the Hop Shop, in Kent, England for supplying the dried flowers used throughout this book.

For Anna, Thom, and Phoebe